Parent's Guide to

iPHONE
& iPAD

ANDREW GERTIG & ANDREW WEILER

For our children,
and yours.

www.mascotbooks.com

Parent's Guide to iPhone® & iPad®

©2017 Andrew Gertig and Andrew Weiler. All Rights Reserved. No part of this publication may be reproduced, stored in a retrieval system or transmitted in any form by any means electronic, mechanical, or photocopying, recording or otherwise without the permission of the author.

Parent's Guide to iPhone & iPad is an independent publication and has not been authorized, sponsored, or otherwise approved by Apple Inc. iPhone and iPad are registered trademarks of Apple Inc.

For more information, please contact:
Mascot Books
560 Herndon Parkway #120
Herndon, VA 20170
info@mascotbooks.com

Library of Congress Control Number: 2016917970

CPSIA Code: PBANG0117A
ISBN-13: 978-1-63177-900-8

Printed in the United States

CONTENTS

GETTING STARTED

As parents and techies ourselves, we at Humans With Kids think it is critical to take a balanced approach towards technology. It is a wonderful tool that can accelerate learning, connect cultures, and develop lasting friendships. It can also ruin lives, destroy families, and wreak havoc on young minds. There are a million statistics that you can find via Google that talk about the benefits and ills of technology usage by children. This book is not intended to make you fear the iPhone and iPad nor is it intended to encourage you to let your child have their own iPhone and iPad and use them however they see fit.

We are realists. We enjoy technology, but we also want the best for our own kids, and yours as well. So, instead of retreating from technology, use this book as the cheat sheet to understand exactly how to leverage your iPhone or iPad for good and mitigate the potential dangers and pitfalls they might present.

We don't think any amount of restriction or control can be more effective than open and honest conversation with your children. Please be sure to have honest conversations with your kids about their internet usage. Set transparency as the norm when it comes to gadgets; it will be far less awkward to intrude later once they have already developed habits. From the beginning, establish the standard that you have as their parent ultimately own and have access to iPhones and iPads they use.

This guide is not a comprehensive look at every feature of the iPhone and iPad. This is an intentional guide to walk parents through the aspects of these devices that we think are most important to understand as a parent, and the features that will most benefit them in their parenting journey. It is also not a comprehensive guide to social media and every app available. If you are like us, you will use this mostly as a reference. There may be an issue that crops up with social media, and you would want to address it. We hope that you can easily find the topic and chapter you need and implement it without having to shuffle around.

For more great stuff related to parenting check out our blog at humanswithkids.com

And finally, remember that your kids will do what you do, more than what you say. If you can never put your phone down at the dinner table don't expect them to either. When you establish rules, make them apply to everyone in the family. Your kids will be more likely to respect your actions than listen to empty words.

We believe being a human with kids and being a parent are two different experiences. Sure, most people have the ability to make a kid, but becoming a parent takes work, intentionality, purpose, and care. In the world today, one of the most treacherous topics to navigate around is technology. Is it good or bad? Should my kid have access? How often? How long? How in the world do I use this thing that is already intuitive to my son or daughter? We have wrestled a lot with these questions and we want to help. We have some suggestions based on actual conversations we have had with parents who have children of all ages. We also want to share our expertise on how to actually accomplish some of these tasks on specific devices, in this case, the iPhone and iPad.

Before we dive in too deep, a quick word to you as a parent about online interactions and social media in general. **You are more of an expert than you think you are.**

While it may be true that you don't know all the ins and outs of an iPhone or an iPad, your experience in life and with people is far greater than your children. You understand how people work, you have hunches and intuitions that are often correct. The world of social media is nothing more than digitized psychology. People are still acting in the ways they have always acted.

Think back to high school. Chances are there were more than a few times where you and a group of friends hung out in a parking lot for a while. You did this because that is where all your friends were, no one could really make a decision about where to go or what to do, and hardly anyone had money to do anything anyway. So, eventually a few kids started doing something silly and kinda dumb, but everyone was laughing. A few other kids wandered away and maybe tried smoking or something else a bit unwholesome. Maybe a fight broke out once in a while, or a bully pushed some people around. A couple maybe snuck over to make out in a car, but by and large, the majority of kids just stood around and talked and laughed.

Social media is just a giant version of that parking lot. Some of the fringe people are a bit weirder, and some people are into some dangerous things, but most everyone is just hanging out and talking about the same stuff you did in that parking lot. You navigated that pretty well, so help your kids navigate their new world well. Ironically, your parents most likely had less opportunity to actively influence your actions back then compared to how close we can be to our kids online. You know how people are, what makes them act in certain ways. Help your children navigate the psychology of human behavior online and you will help them more in the long run than any tip or trick we can give you.

Secondly, you are raising an adult, not a child. Imagine a circle. Your child is living inside that circle and you are the one who has created the boundary. Eventually, that boundary will cease to exist. As a parent, your job is to constantly expand or contract that boundary to fit in line with your child's growth. In general, it should be just tight enough that your child can see the edge and is thinking about what is outside and maybe feeling like it is just a hair too small in their minds. For you, it should feel a hair too wide, enough that you constantly want to go check that they haven't crossed over the edge. That delicate balance is why parents get gray hair and furrowed brows. In the arena of technology, this becomes increasingly import-ant, because most of our kids are native users, so it is to be expected that we would feel more angst parenting on the edge with a tool we aren't quite as comfortable with. Hopefully, this book helps you feel equipped to wade in and help your child navigate the world of technology, spe-cifically as they use an iPhone or iPad.

TECHNOLOGY IS MORALLY NEUTRAL

There is nothing inherently good or bad about technolo-gy. It is a tool that can be put to both good and evil uses, but nothing about its nature is inherently evil. Technology can open windows to things that none of us want our chil-dren to see, it can connect them to people who we would never want them connected, and it can sometimes cause them to forsake good activity for static entertainment. However, the opposites can also be true. They can have their eyes opened to exciting new ideas, they can connect with friends and loved ones who are far away, and they can learn and share the best of what they are doing.

Using technology is like driving a car. As a child, you think that driving is simple and exciting. As a teenager, you are foolishly certain that you are a good driver, but as an adult you appreciate the responsibility and are well aware of the dangers. Technology for kids is pretty simple and exciting. Teens think they are masters despite the evidence to the contrary, and parents just want everyone to stay safe.

Human nature is really the thing all parents are worried about. The desire to gratify ones own self above all else can be accomplished with relative ease through technology. As parents, one of our biggest challenges is to help our kids break out of that habit and become a highly functioning human being that makes a positive impact in the world. Technology can help in that cause as much as it hurts. Being a great parent means wading into all the spaces your kids are in and helping them learn how to operate properly.

TECHNOLOGY IS HERE TO STAY

There is no denying the world we live in, and technology is only becoming more ubiquitous. People will interact more and more seamlessly with computers in the years to come. There is no going backwards on this. Think about a world where the progress of transportation was intentionally reversed. It's not going to happen. The same is true with our computers and mobile devices. It just isn't going to start going backwards.

So, what do we do about all this technology, especially these devices like iPhones and iPads that are with us all the time, always seem to be on, and forever draw our attention?

We believe that these mobile devices feel extra personal, but we should bring them into the light. They cannot stay hidden. A cell phone is not a diary. It is not a personal journal with a lock and key that no one should access, but sometimes they feel that way. Social media is shared with the whole world, and yet sometimes kids want to keep what they do online hidden. That is the biggest mistake they make. Nothing online is really hidden, it is all viewed, tracked, clicked and stored. The illusion of privacy comes from the feeling that our device is only ours and that we control all the things associated with it. That is not true, and we need to help our children realize this, and more importantly, we can invade that space a little as well. It isn't to say that they can have no trust from you as they use the device, but we mustn't let our kids grow up thinking that they have private room to view the world. In reality, it is more like sitting in a glass house into which everyone can see.

AVOID THESE 7 DIGITAL SINS

COMPLACENCY

Don't get caught thinking that because things are going well now, that all will stay well. Social media and device usage is a constant ebb and flow. Your child might be incredibly responsible, but that doesn't mean you shouldn't regularly check up on them. You need to ask what they are watching, reading and posting online. Growing up, my mother used to tell me that I should never think that I was the type of person who could never get caught up in bad actions or behavior. This attitude is helpful to teach your kids. They can always be tempted by images and ideas. They, and us as parents, need to remember that pitfalls can always lay around the next corner.

CONFORMITY

Don't get caught believing that because all the other families you know are allowing a certain behavior that you must allow it as well. For instance, most social media sites require users to be at least 13 before participating. You can choose to enforce that or not. Many parents choose to allow their children access to that world before age 13. It is okay to set your own time line and limits for your children. Your kids might not like it, but you are the parent, and your judgment should not be swayed by every other parent on the block. Of course, you should have a conversation with your kids about what you believe and why so that they at least have context for your decision, and don't avoid technology forever, but feel free to set the right limits.

LATE ADOPTION

This one comes right after conformity because sometimes parents just don't care to keep up with the latest social trends. That's fine, but if your kids are curious, you better be curious as well. Don't be the last one to the party on the next social media app or device because it will only make it harder for you to help your kids navigate the nuances of whatever app or device they are on next. If staying up to date is hard for you, then ask your kids what is next, or what they hear of friends using and go figure out those ones. There is no need to know everything, just the ones that are pertinent to your kids.

NOSTALGIA

Things were so much better back in the day, right? Wrong, if you are a child or especially a teenager. One day, this will be their good old days too. It has always been that way. We all look back on our collective past with rose colored glasses. More importantly though is that when you tell your kids that you can't stand what they are interested in today, you create a larger gap for you to cross when you want to engage them. You don't have to be a social media wizard, and there is no need for you to be the most adept at the latest online game. Instead, you need to understand that these are the things that your kids are excited about, and when you shut down the conversation, they stop talking to you about it. That is the thing you want to avoid wholeheartedly. Keep the conversation open!

ISOLATION

While mobile devices feel intensely personal, they shouldn't be used exclusively alone. Instead, it should be normal at your house for people to see and have access to all devices. Long stretches of time alone with a device isn't healthy for any of us. Make it normal to show your phone and to check in on what is happening on your child's device as well.

GLUTTONY

Too much is never good. One great rule of thumb we have come across is that you should have an hour every day, and a day every week, and a week every year completely away from any type of technology. That is wise. Being too plugged in and too dependent are going to cause us problems. When your child's world gets consumed by being online and connected, it is important to remind them that there are many other valuable pursuits for their time.

HYPOCRISY

Lastly, hypocrisy. Yes, so very often we make rules that we don't want to apply to us. We choose to not allow any phones at the dinner table except ours. We choose to make our kids show us their devices and pictures but keep ours hidden. In this world, it should be a two-way street. Play by your own rules. Model the right behavior and be willing to show restraint yourself. If you really inventory your time, you might be surprised by how much you are glued to your own device.

INSTEAD OF COMMITTING THESE DIGITAL SINS, TRY INSTEAD TO...

BE INVOLVED

One of the best analogies of parenting I have heard is that kids are like puppies when they are young. They love you, snuggle up to you, and are generally so far involved in your business that sometimes you need to hide away. Then as your kids grow into teens they become like cats. They barely tolerate your presence except for those few moments when they decide that they want to rub up against you and be given some attention. Stay involved. Cherish the moments when they are young and pour your knowledge in when they are open to it. As they grow, be clued into the moments when they are open to you and jump on them. Ask questions, be connected to their lives, find out what they are into and connect.

BE UNDERSTANDING

It isn't always easy being a kid. Take the time to understand where they are coming from and why they want to use a device, an app or a game. You may not see the value at first, and truthfully not everything has value, but sometimes they are able to open our eyes to new and valuable tools. Also, try to understand what is happening in your child's online sphere. If they are experiencing some positive friendships or new learning then be encouraged. It is possible that they may experience bullying, friends that are depressed or anxious, and many other negative emotions. Be sure to connect and seek to understand what is going on in their online worlds. So many young people will share deep thoughts, feelings, and fears online that they won't tell their closest family or friends. Be the place where they can share that with you. Extend grace when it is needed.

BE PROGRESSIVE

Let your rules evolve and grow with your children. Set up rules or boundaries, but recognize when they have outgrown them and are ready for new responsibility. Maybe you have lots of restrictions when they are young, then slowly relax them. Maybe this is an order that you allow your kids to use social media apps. With new apps coming out all the time, you will have to stay in touch with what is happening and adjust accordingly.

BE CONSISTENT

In your character and in your application of the rules, be sure to follow through and be true to your own family values. Don't get caught bending the rules yourself. Also, be consistent between kids. Younger siblings often end up with access at an earlier age than older siblings. This happens partly because of the older child, but also because we get conditioned to feel okay with something after we are around it for a while. If your older child had to wait to get a device, think hard about whether the younger one should have one before that same age. Sometimes the changing nature of technology or even of education dictates that these changes happen, but be consistent when you can and then give your kids context to your decisions as those decisions evolve.

BE FEARLESS

I dread the day I have to ask my daughter a question like, "Have you ever sent a naked picture of yourself to someone?" Direct questions are scary. It feels much easier to say things like, "Are you using your iPad appropriately?" Those questions are generally useless. Asking open ended questions to generate a discussion is great, but vague statements that help you feel good about checking in are not. Direct questions are much harder to dodge and evade, and they are easier to discern the truth. Just don't become the CIA interrogator. Have a delicate balance searching for the truth and showing your children grace.

Here are a few best practices that might help guide your family decisions on technology use.

1. Make a point to understand the device or app your child wants to use. Don't be caught in the dark.

2. Interact with your kids via the apps they use, such as Facebook, Instagram, Snapchat. If you let them be on it, then you be on it, and not just as the police. Actually interact in positive ways too.

3. Don't give full access too soon. Set up some healthy restrictions.

4. Don't force them to hide from you. Over-restricting can sometimes cause as many problems as under-restricting. Set up reasonable restrictions and limits.

5. Charge their device in another room, even if it might require you to buy them an alarm clock. Your grandma said nothing good happened after midnight. The same rule applies online.

6. Anonymous and hidden apps are unwise. Any app that allows you to not be you or that is designed to hide your activity is probably going to get you into trouble.

7. Challenge your kids to use social media as a platform

for doing good. Let them live out the best of your family values online, not the worst.

8. Inspect what you expect when it comes to online behavior.

9. Give context to your decisions, even when it falls on deaf ears.

10. Ask direct questions. Do not settle for vague questions or responses.

After using our iPhones and iPads with our own children and working in children's ministry ranging from preschool to high school, we have learned that there are some common things that parents wish they knew how to do with their iPhones and iPads. Recipes are simple step-by-step instructions, with pictures, on how to accomplish these tasks. Feel free to jump to the ones you care about; we have done our best to allow each recipe to stand alone and will point you to other sections of the book that may be relevant to what you are reading.

We promise this is going to be much easier than you think, and remember, you can always come back to this book to brush up!

HOW TO
Lock the Settings on your iPhone or iPad

This recipe is all about creating a **Restrictions Passcode**. This is a foundational recipe as many of the other recipes in this book build upon it. It will teach you how to lock many if not most of your device's important settings so that they cannot be changed without your **Restrictions Passcode**.

LOCKING THE SETTINGS?

Locking the Settings means that you "**Enable Restrictions**" on your device. Enabling **Restrictions** just means that you now have the ability restrict certain features and settings on your device. We cover each one of these in our chapter about **Restrictions**. In order to **Enable Restrictions** you must create a **Restrictions Passcode** and that is what this recipe will teach you.

WAIT, THERE IS MORE THAN ONE KIND OF PASSCODE?

In this book we talk about three different types of Passcodes that you can have on your iPhone or iPad. They are: **Device Passcode** (Apple calls this just a Passcode), **Restrictions Passcode**, and **Guided Access Passcode**. Here is a quick summary of what each of these is:

- **Device Passcode** – this is the passcode you use to unlock your iPhone after it goes to sleep. Typically it is a 4 or 6 digit code though some people prefer to enable the full text option for their passcode (we don't think that's really necessary). Devices that have **Touch ID** allow you to use your fingerprint to unlock your device rather than typing in your passcode.

- **Restrictions Passcode** – this is the 4 or 6 digit passcode that you use to lock the **Restrictions** on your device and is the passcode we are addressing in this recipe.

- **Guided Access Passcode** – this is the 4 or 6 digit passcode for locking Guided Access. We teach you all about Guided Access in the recipe: How to Keep Your Child from Exiting an App.

Each of these passcodes can be different from the others. Our recommendation is that you make your **Restrictions Passcode** and **Guided Access Passcode** the same 4 or 6 digit code but make your **Device Passcode** different. For example, if your **Device Passcode** is 123456 then your **Restrictions Passcode** could be 566832 and your **Guided Access Passcode** would also be 566832. We think that this is a good idea as you may want your child to be able to unlock an iPhone or iPad but don't want them to be able to modify the **Settings** on that device.

SETTING UP YOUR RESTRICTIONS PASSCODE

First tap on the **Settings** icon on your Home screen then tap on **General** then on **Restrictions**.

Then tap on **Enable Restrictions**.

Then enter a 4-digit passcode you would like to use as your **Restrictions Passcode** and confirm it. Remember that this should be different from your **Device Passcode**!

●●○○○ Verizon 📶 11:51 PM 100% 🔋⚡	●●○○○ Verizon 📶 11:52 PM 100% 🔋⚡
Set Passcode Cancel	**Set Passcode** Cancel
Enter a Restrictions Passcode	Re-enter your Restrictions Passcode
— — — —	● — — —
Remember to make this different than your unlock passcode	
1 2 ABC 3 DEF	1 2 ABC 3 DEF
4 GHI 5 JKL 6 MNO	4 GHI 5 JKL 6 MNO
7 PQRS 8 TUV 9 WXYZ	7 PQRS 8 TUV 9 WXYZ

You have now successfully **Enabled Restrictions**! Many of the other recipes in this book teach you about the settings and features that you can now manage through the Restrictions menu. Read on to the next recipe to put what you have just learned into practice

HOW TO

Restrict Explicit Content

If we can help it, we all want to keep our children from being exposed to content that they just should not see. This recipe allows you to restrict **Explicit Content** on your iPhone and iPad. This recipe is predicated on setting up a **Restrictions Passcode**, so if you haven't done that take a look at the How to Lock the Settings on your iPhone or iPad recipe.

Restricting **Explicit Content** is not a failsafe plan to keep all adult material off of your devices. This recipe will help you keep your kids from navigating to any **Explicit Sexual Content** within a web browser, and we tested with more than just Safari, Apple's proprietary browser. The filter does a good job, and gives you the option to allow sites with your **Restrictions Passcode** if you decide they should be viewable. However, having open conversations with your children about language and content choices is imperative. Also, even if you limit the content that you can download with Apple, not every App has the same limits. For instance, limiting **Movies** and **TV Shows** has no bearing on what you can watch in Netflix.

LIMITING ADULT CONTENT

The **Explicit Content** filter options are located inside **Restrictions**. Tap on the **Settings** icon from your **Home Screen**. Then, tap on **General**. Next, tap **Restrictions.**

Enter your **Restrictions Passcode**, then scroll down and you will find a section labeled **"Allowed Content."**

●○○○○ Verizon 🔋 10:12 PM ⊙ 99% ▭✦
Enter Passcode Cancel
Enter your Restrictions Passcode
— — — —
1	2 ABC	3 DEF
4 GHI	5 JKL	6 MNO
7 PQRS	8 TUV	9 WXYZ
	0	⌫

●○○○○ Verizon 🔋 12:20 AM 100% ▭✦
‹ General **Restrictions**
ALLOWED CONTENT:
Ratings For United States ›
Music, Podcasts & iTunes U Clean ›
Movies PG-13 ›
TV Shows TV-14 ›
Books Restricted ›
Apps All ›
Siri All ›
Websites Restricted ›
PRIVACY:
Location Services ›

In this recipe we specifically look at **Websites**, but you can see a more comprehensive look at all the **Restrictions** in our chapter dedicated to them. Or just tap each row and explore. Tap on **Websites** and then choose the option that works best for your family. We recommend selecting **Limit Adult Content**. This will limit many websites, even ones that you or your child may not consider inappropriate. You will need a passcode to allow those sites, but once they are allowed they go in a managed list you can find under **Always Allow**. Conversely, if there are sites you know you do not want your children accessing, you can add them to the **Never Allow** section to permanently restrict access.

Congratulations! You have successfully **Limited Adult Content**. Don't forget to adjust the settings of the other options in **Allowed Content**. For a more in-depth look at all the **Restrictions** options, check out our chapter on **Restrictions**.

HOW TO
Disable Downloading Apps and Music

I can get it just 'cause I want it, right Dad? Not so fast. Sometimes we don't want our kids downloading and installing something on a device without our knowledge, and sometimes those things cost money, and that money comes out of our pockets. There are two ways to think about this. The first is to manage purchases only through **Family Sharing**. If you need help setting up family sharing and enabling **Ask to Buy** follow the recipe: *How to Share Purchases Using Family Sharing*. This recipe allows you to actually restrict **Installing Apps**. Located in the same area are **Deleting Apps, In-App Purchases**, and several other options. Take a look at our comprehensive look at **Restrictions** if you want to learn about each of these specifically.

TURN OFF INSTALLING APPS

This recipe will walk you through turning off **Installing Apps**. This will prevent anyone from downloading an app onto your device. This is particularly helpful if you have a child in one of those fun games that has ads asking them to download another App. They find themselves out of the App they were in and browsing the App Store. Everything looks fun to little fingers and before you know it, you have one of everything. You can also lock your kids into one App by following our recipe on *How to Keep your Child from Exiting an App*.

Tap on the **Settings** icon and tap **General**. After that, scroll down and tap **Restrictions** where you will be prompted to enter your **Restrictions Passcode**. This bears repeating, but you ought to set up a **Restrictions Passcode**, and it should be different than your **Device Passcode**. To learn more about why and how to set up your **Restrictions Passcode** see our recipe *How to Lock the Settings on your iPhone or iPad*.

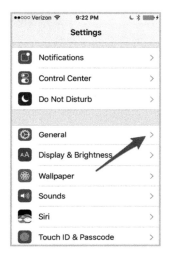

Scroll down a bit and you will see a section starting with **iTunes Store** (sliding that to off will disallow downloads from the iTunes store, disabling the ability to download music, but not listening to Apple Music). Find and slide **Installing Apps** to off.

That's it! You have now disabled **Installing Apps**. We also recommend turning off **In-App Purchases** if you don't want to buy a bunch of extra paid content inside of an App or Game.

HOW TO
Keep the Volume From Getting Too Loud

Sometimes as a parent you may want to let your child listen to music, an app, or watch a video on your iPhone or iPad. If you have ever cranked up the volume on your device, you know that it can be way too loud. Thankfully Apple allows us to limit the maximum volume on our iOS devices, allowing us to prevent children from turning up the volume to a point that could damage their developing ears. Let's jump right in.

SETTING THE MAXIMUM VOLUME

Head to the **Settings** app on your iPhone (could also be your iPad or iPod touch, it's all the same, but from here we will just refer to your iPhone). You might guess that the **Max Volume** setting would be under the **Sounds** menu but that's not actually where it's hidden. You have to go to the **Music** menu item:

Then tap **Volume Limit** (which probably shows as being Off):

And slide the slider to your preferred **Max Volume**

Unfortunately, as you are changing the **Max Volume** it does not give you an audible way to check what you have changed it to. The best way to check the volume limit is to head to your Music app on that device after setting the limit, and play your favorite song. Then go back to the volume setting if need be and adjust accordingly.

PREVENT ANYONE FROM
CHANGING THE MAXIMUM VOLUME

Now that you have set your preferred **Max Volume** you can now head to the **Restrictions** menu and lock your Music setting for **Max Volume**:

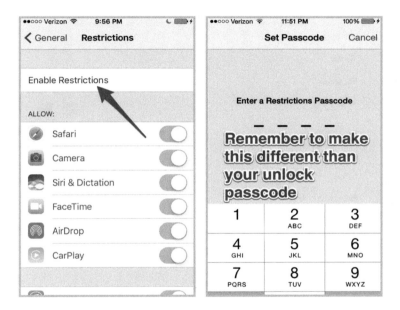

If you are wondering why you should use a separate pass-code for Restrictions than you do for locking your iPhone, you should check out the recipe: *How to Lock the Settings on your iPhone or iPad.*

Next you will need to scroll all the way down to find
Volume Limit:

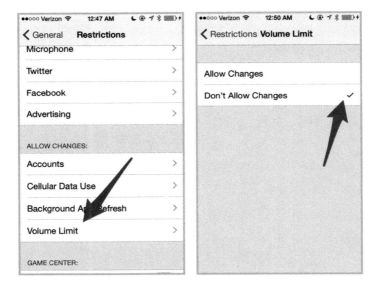

Tap on **Volume Limit** and the select **Don't Allow Changes**.
That's it! Now you know where to find the Volume Limit
setting on your device and how to prevent this from being
changed. Just be careful not to forget about this setting
and begin to think your iPhone is broken because it's "not
loud enough."

HOW TO
Keep Your Child From Exiting an App

This recipe will teach you how to prevent your child from intentionally or accidentally leaving the app you want them to stay in. This is one of our favorite features for our younger children who somehow love to find a way to hit the **Home Button** (Round button at the bottom of the screen) and then get into our email to send very meaningful messages to our bosses. We've all been there, right? Apple has been kind enough to give us a feature called **Guided Access** that allows us to stop this madness. Apple describes it as:

Guided Access helps you to stay focused on a task while using your iPhone, iPad or iPod touch. Guided Access limits your device to a single app and lets you control which app features are available.

To us, that reads as: "Guided Access was a gift to parents so that they don't have to continually help their wonderful children get back into the app they just left."

WHAT ELSE CAN GUIDED ACCESS DO?

Guided Access is very useful and flexible. Besides temporarily locking your device into one app, it can also be used to set up untouchable areas on the screen and can even be used to set a timer on an app so that your child can only use it for however long you choose. You can also disable the **Sleep/Wake Button** at the top of the phone, disable the **Volume Buttons**, disable the ability for the device to detect **Motion** (For example some games detect the movement of the iPhone as a part of the game play), disable the **Keyboard**, or if you feel the need, you can disable **Touch** altogether.

ENABLING GUIDED ACCESS

Guided Access is tucked away under the **Accessibility** settings. Begin by tapping on the **Settings** icon on your Home Screen then tap on **General** and then tap **Accessibility**. Scroll down until you see **Guide Access**, and tap on it.

Turn **Guided Access** on then tap on **Passcode Settings**. This will allow you to set the 4-digit **Guided Access Passcode,** which will prevent your child from being able to exit **Guided Access**.

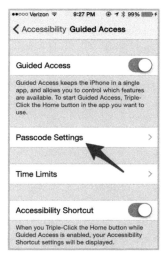

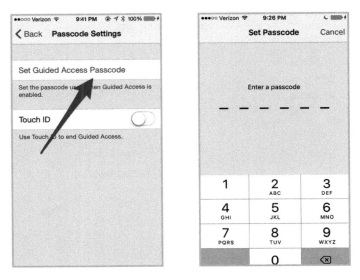

Enter your 4 or 6 digit **Guided Access Passcode** (Remember, a good practice is to make this different from your **Device Passcode**!) and confirm it.

You can enable **Touch ID** here if it is available on your device. We love it. You may have noticed the **Time Limits** option and that **Accessibility Shortcut** is enabled by default. For now, don't worry about these options. The only thing **Time Limits** does in this menu is allow you to change the sound that gets played when a time limit is reached.

USING GUIDED ACCESS

Now that you have **Guided Access** set up and ready to go it is time to use it! Starting **Guided Access** can be a little tricky at first but you will get used to it, I promise. The first step is to go to your Home Screen and find an app that you want your child to stay in. Tap on the app's icon. Now, in order to access **Guided Access,** you must **triple tap** on the **Home Button**. If you hit those taps just right, you should see something that looks like this:

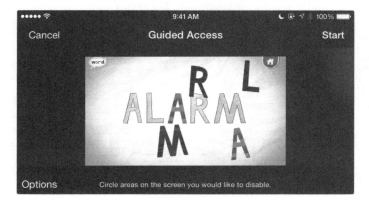

If you accidentally did a double tap instead of a triple tap you will see the App Switcher view which will look something like this. Not to fear, just tap on the icon for the app you want and try again.

Once you get the triple click down you should see a zoomed out version of the app you were in.

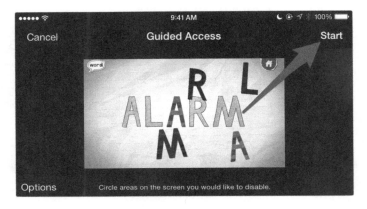

From this view, you can Start **Guided Access** by tapping the **Start** button. If you want to check to see if it worked, just try tapping the **Home Button** one time to go back to the Home Screen. You shouldn't be able to! And should see a banner at the top of the screen telling you that **Guided Access** in enabled.

Now that you have figured out how to Enable **Guided Access**, let's try ending it.

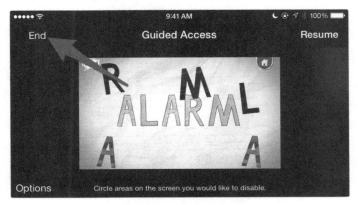

To do this, triple click the **Home Button** again then type in your **Guided Access Passcode** and you will be brought back to the zoomed out screen. Tap the **End Button** to end **Guided Access**.

ADDITIONAL WAYS TO USE GUIDED ACCESS

As we mentioned earlier there are a few other things you can accomplish with Guided Access. One of the most useful is the ability to block off certain parts of the screen that you might not want your child to touch like advertisements or buttons that take them out of the gameplay. You can also do things like disabling the **Sleep/Wake Button** so that the phone can't be put to sleep accidentally with an errant bump. Similarly you can disable the **Volume Buttons** so that the volume of an app cannot be changed. Other things that you can disable are the detection of **Motion**, **Keyboards,** and any **Touch** on the screen. This last one is not something you would really need to disable as it is intended for when the device is being used as a demo unit. You can see the Options view below.

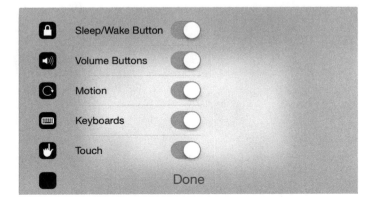

DISABLING AREAS ON THE SCREEN

The other options are just toggle switches but this option requires a little more than that. In order to create areas that are disabled on a screen you will need to be in the zoomed out view. The first step is to use your finger to draw an outline around the area you would like to disable. Make sure that you connect the lines you draw or else they will not stay. If you successfully draw an outline you will see a grayed out area with an **X Button (Close)** and a series of dots around the edges. You can use the dots to resize the area by tapping and dragging on them. You can also shift the area around.

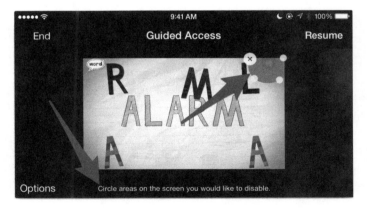

Once you are satisfied you can then tap **Start** or **Resume** depending on whether you have already started **Guided Access** and then you should see the area you disabled shown and you shouldn't be able to tap on it anymore. Sometimes in children's games the touchable area is actually larger than the outline of the button and so it is a good idea to make the disabled area larger than the button itself to ensure that you have indeed disabled it.

Whew that was a lot of **Guided Access** and triple tapping! Now you can go back to preparing dinner and not worry about your little one being frustrated or getting into apps they shouldn't.

HOW TO

Approve Purchases

Even when we trust our kids, we don't always give them carte blanche with our credit card. There is a simple fix implemented by Apple with **Family Sharing**. You can add each member of your family under your **Family Sharing** plan, and then set each person with either the ability to **Approve Purchases** or make them **Ask to Buy**. If you need to set up Family Sharing, follow the *How to Share Purchases with Your Family* recipe.

This recipe will help you set up the **Ask to Buy** feature ensuring that, before any purchase, you are able to approve that purchase. This is a great feature to leave on as your kids are younger, and then bestow upon them as a privilege as they get older, and prove to be more responsible.

Also, you can set other Parents/Guardians with the ability to approve purchases as well. That means that both parents can have the ability to approve a purchase, not just the family **Organizer.**

Ask to Buy is only an available feature on accounts for family members under 18, and you can only have 5 members plus the organizer for a total of 6 **Family Members**. In other words, if Grandma is on your **Family Sharing Plan**, she can buy as many versions of cribbage as she wants on your dime, so choose wisely.

HOW TO TURN ON ASK TO BUY

Tap the **Settings** icon, scroll down and tap on the **iCloud**. This will take you to a screen where you can manage your **iCloud** account as well as your family members.

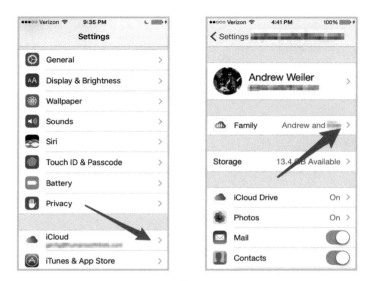

Tap on **Family** and then tap on the name of the **Family Member** that you want to manage. Make sure to slide **Ask to Buy** on and you are ready to approve all of that **Family Member's** purchases.

HOW TO

Set Up Do Not Disturb

Do Not Disturb is a feature that keeps calls and alerts like text messages and Facebook posts from showing up on your phone until you turn **Do Not Disturb** off. You can also configure it to create a short list of people who are able to break through the do not disturb status. As a parent, we think that this is an important feature to understand, but you will need to have a conversation with your child because this can't be parentally locked. That means you can talk about how you expect this to be set up and then inspect from time to time, but you can't lock it. Remember that your inspections shouldn't always be punitive or suspicious in nature. If you check and everything is the way you expect it to be, make sure to encourage your child and maybe even reward them for being responsible. Also, remember that **Do Not Disturb** only disables audible notifications. Text messages will show up on the screen, for instance, but the phone will not chime or vibrate as an indicator.

RECOMMENDED SETTINGS

We recommend the following settings be applied as well as these guidelines for use.

If your child takes their phone to school, schedule **Do Not Disturb** for school hours. We all know how tempting it is to read a text or check a status when we are alerted, so set **Do Not Disturb** for school hours to reduce the temptation to check or interrupt a class. For students, we recommend just using the manual switch when going to bed and then turning it off when they wake up. You can also turn off the scheduling for the weekend so they have access.

Additionally, and this recommendation goes for parents as well, turn on **Do Not Disturb** when you get in the car. You can specify important contacts that can break through by setting **Favorites**, but it will help you not get distracted by text messages or random calls that come in and cause you to scramble around looking for your phone or finding your bluetooth.

Leaving on **Repeated Calls** is fine unless you find that your child is abusing that feature by having friends just call twice.

Also, keep **Silence** on **Always**, so that even if they happen to be looking at their phone, the **Do Not Disturb** settings will remain in effect.

You can quickly check your child's phone by seeing the **Moon Icon** in the **Status Bar**. Maybe a quick check and reminder when you drop them off, or before they get ready to drive somewhere will help ensure that they remember.

SETTING UP DO NOT DISTURB

Tap the **Settings** icon. From there, scroll down and tap the blue moon icon with **Do Not Disturb** written beside it.

To set the schedule, slide **Scheduled** to on. Then you will have the option to choose from which time to which time the **Do Not Disturb** settings should be applied.

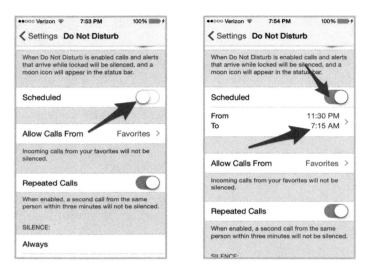

Next, tap **Allow Calls From**. It will send you to another menu that allows you to pick which people can break the **Do Not Disturb**. The default option is **Favorites.** We recommend leaving this option or selecting **No One**. There is a way to create a family group, but that is more trouble than it's worth.

Also, slide **Repeated Calls** to on and Tap **Silence Always**.
If you leave **Only When Phone is Locked,** then any time
you are looking at the phone, alerts will sound.

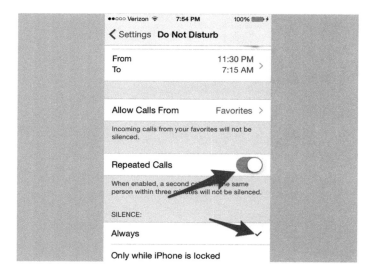

Of course, **Do Not Disturb** is a great feature for yourself
as well. You can use it to avoid that awkward moment in
a meeting when you have set your phone to vibrate and
then set it on the table only to have it rattle and echo
through the entire meeting five minutes later. It is also
a great way to help you avoid the temptation to look at
texts while driving. It can even be used at the dinner table
by everyone to avoid getting distracted and engage in
the conversation. To quickly and easily enable or disable
Do Not Disturb, swipe up from the bottom to access the
Control Center and tap the Moon icon.

Go forth and enjoy your newfound quiet!

HOW TO
Find Your Child Using Find My iPhone

Have you tried yelling? Just kidding! This recipe will teach you how to use the powerful features that Apple provides for you to be able to locate an iPhone or iPad using GPS or Wi-Fi determined location. <u>Note:</u> We highly recommend having an open discussion with your child about why you think this is important.

In order to track the location of an iPhone or iPad, we will teach you about the two apps provided by Apple that allow this functionality. This chapter focuses on the **Find My iPhone** app.

This might sound a little confusing at first, but **Find My iPhone** is a feature built into the operating system **and** an app you can download from the App Store. The **Find My iPhone** app does not need to be installed on the device you wish to track for this recipe to work. Nor do you need it installed on your own device to be able to view the location of another device. The app is just useful for quickly being able to see the locations of the devices in your family without having to go to **iCloud.com** in a web browser. We recommend that you only download the **Find My iPhone** app on your own device, not on the iPhone or iPad that your child will be using.

TURNING ON FIND MY IPHONE

Before you are able to locate an iPhone or iPad you will need to make a few changes if you have not already done so. The following steps are to be performed on the iPhone or iPad that you wish to locate.

First, you must be signed in to **iCloud** on your child's device. You can check whether you are by tapping on the **Settings** app and then scrolling down and tapping on iCloud. You are probably already signed in to iCloud, but if not, go ahead and do so.

Once you are signed in, scroll down and make sure that **Find My iPhone** is turned on.

Now you are ready to start tracking this device's location!

PREVENT FIND MY IPHONE FROM BEING DISABLED

Of course your angel would never try to disable this feature, but just in case they were to ever **accidentally** try to do so, you can use **Restrictions** to ensure they cannot turn **Find My iPhone** off. If you have not yet enabled Restrictions you can learn how by following the *How to Lock the Settings on your iPhone or iPad* recipe.

Once you have **Enabled Restrictions,** you can now scroll down and tap on **Location Services** then tap on **Don't Allow Changes.**

Optional step: Scroll all the way down and tap on **Find My iPhone** and make sure that it is On and that the Status Bar Icon is Off.

Now make sure that **Don't Allow Changes** has a check mark next to it. This will prevent your child from turning off the Find My iPhone feature without the Restrictions Passcode.

Now celebrate, you have discovered how to control aspects of your device without prying fingers coming after you and undoing your hard work.

VIEW YOUR CHILD'S LOCATION ON A MAP

There are two ways to view your child's location on a map, and both ways require you to know the iCloud username and password associated with the device you wish to track. The first way is to use the **Find My iPhone** app that you can download from the App Store onto your iPhone or iPad. The other way is to use the website **iCloud.com**. Here we will cover how to find a device using the web browser on your computer.

Navigate to **http://icloud.com/find** and login with the iCloud account used to set up **Find My iPhone** on the child's device. You should now see a map showing all the devices associated with that iCloud account.

To see only one device, select **All Devices** and choose the device you are interested in.

Now you will be able to see the last known location of your child's iPhone or iPad!

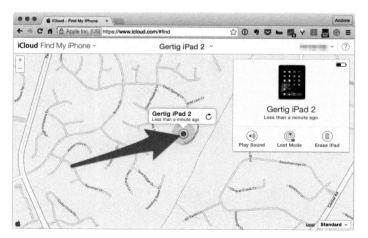

BONUS: MAKE AN IPHONE OR IPAD BEEP LOUDLY USING FIND MY IPHONE

This feature is intended to help you find your iPhone if it is lost somewhere, like in the couch cushions, but you can use it for a little bit of teaching too if you see fit. Tapping on the **Play Sound** button will cause the iPhone or iPad to Beep loudly even if the sound is turned off on the device. Use this as you see fit!

This bonus feature is useful for a myriad of purposes so don't forget about it!

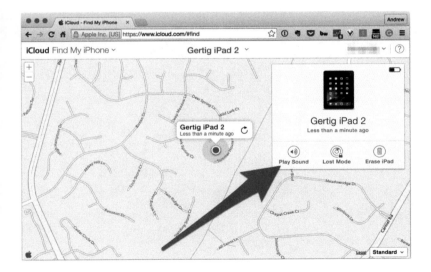

HOW TO

Find Your Child Using Find My Friends

This recipe will teach you how to use the powerful features that Apple provides for you to be able to locate an iPhone or iPad using a GPS or Wi-Fi determined location. <u>Note:</u> We highly recommend having an open discussion with your child about why you think this is important.

In order to track the location of an iPhone or iPad, we will teach you about the two apps provided by Apple that allow this functionality. This chapter focuses on the **Find My Friends** app. Please note that this functionality has changed between iOs 10 and earlier versions. We have included both and noted them accordingly in case you have not upgraded yet, or have an older device for your child.

Apple has been working to turn the **Find My Friends** app into the best way for families and friends to know where each other are. **Find My Friends** has the added feature that Apple calls geofences. A geofence is a circular "fence" around a location and the phone will detect whether or not you are entering or leaving the circle. You can use geofences to send notifications for when your child is leaving or arriving at a location. The difference between iOS 9 and iOS 10 is that in iOS 9 you can request to follow someone without sharing your location. In iOS 10 you must volunteer your location and then the other person will share their location back with you. The best way to make this work is by setting it up on your child's device and sharing the location with your own device.

The **Find My Friends** app does not come pre-installed, so it should be downloaded from the App Store. Unlike **Find My iPhone**, both devices, yours and your child's should have the app installed on them for this recipe to work best. **Find My Friends** is not affected by **Find My iPhone** but is affected by **Share My Location**. If you set up **Family Sharing** each Family member will automatically have **Share My Location** turned on and they will show up in **Find My Friends** without needing to invite them. If you haven't set up Family Sharing check out our recipe dedicated to it: *How to Share Purchases Using Family Sharing*.

To double check that it is, go to **Settings** then tap on **iCloud** then scroll down and tap on **Share My Location** and ensure the switch is on.

In **iOS 10**, this can also be done inside the **Find My Friends** app.

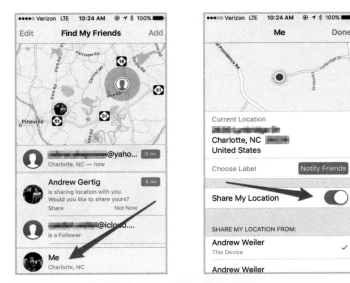

GETTING STARTED

If you are using **Family Sharing** when you open the app you should see a list of your family members and you can skip the next few steps related to inviting friends to use **Find My Friends**.

If you are not using it, then to get started open the **Find My Friends** app and tap on the **Add Button**.

If you are using **iOS 10**, we suggest you use your child's device. This will give you the opportunity to accept or decline sharing back with them. If you are glad to share your location with your child, then you can follow these steps on your device. If you would prefer to not share your location with your child, you should follow these steps on your child's device.

INVITING FRIENDS IN IOS 9

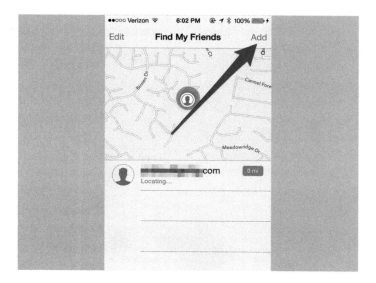

Start typing the name of your child if they are a contact in your phone (ensure their iCloud ID is in their contacts) or email address of the iCloud account. In this example Andrew Gertig will be the parent and will be tracking the location of Andrew Weiler, who is the child in this scenario. You can select the person from the list. To invite via just an email address, make sure you hit the **Return** button on the Keyboard to turn the address Orange so that you can then hit the Done button to send the invite.

Once you the send the invite, the person you invited will see the invitation on their lock screen or within the app if it is open. This is where **iOS 9** and **iOS 10** operate differently. Below is the operation in **iOS 9.**

Inside the app the child will have the option to Accept or Decline the invitation. Tap on **Accept** after either hitting Close or View.

When **Accept** is tapped on the child's (Andrew Weiler) device the parent (Andrew Gertig) will receive a notification that says that the Friend request was accepted. You can tap on **Close** and then **Decline** if you do not wish for your child to be able to view your location within this app. You can, of course, choose to **Accept** if it is okay with you.

INVITING FRIENDS IN IOS 10.

Here are those same steps in **iOS 10.** Remember, in this scenario, we recommend going through these steps on your child's device. In this example, Andrew Gertig will be the parent and will be tracking the location of Andrew Weiler, who is the child in this scenario. This means, he is using Andrew Weiler's device to set up **Find My Friends.**

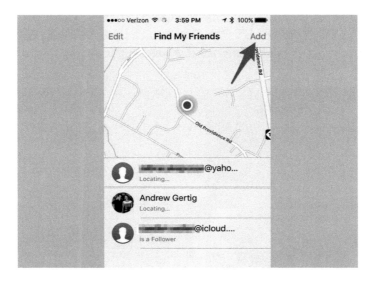

Start typing your name if you are a contact in their phone (ensure their iCloud ID is in their contacts) or email address of the iCloud account. You can select the person from the list. To invite via just an email address, make sure you hit the **Return** button on the Keyboard to turn the address Orange so that you can then hit the Done button to send the invite.

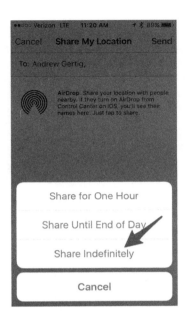

Once you have selected yourself, click on the amount of time you wish to have this information. For younger children, you can go ahead and click "Share Indefinitely" but if you have older children, you may want to use this by sharing different amounts of time based on the level of responsibility they have been showing. This is an opportunity to reward them with some trust as they prove themselves.

Once you have shared your child's location, you will get confirmation on their device that they have started sharing location with you.

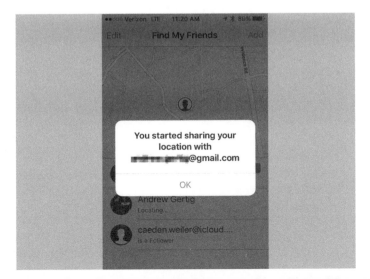

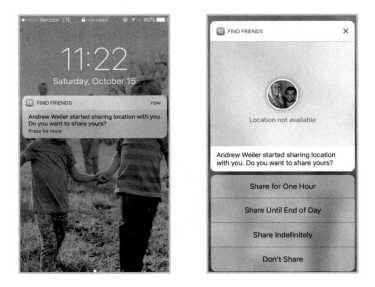

You will receive a notification on your phone, either on your lock screen or inside the app informing you that they have shared their location with you. Inside the app you will have the option to Accept or Decline the invitation to share your location with your child. Tap on the amount of time you would like to share your location.

CREATING A GEOFENCE NOTIFICATION IN IOS 10.

There are slight differences in the way this works between **iOS 9** and **iOS 10.** What follows immediately are the steps in **iOS 10.** Following that, you will see the section on how to do this in **iOS 9**.

Now that you have "**Friends**" you can now set up geofence notifications. To get started open **Find My Friends** on your iPhone and tap on their name (Note: the parent in this example is Andrew Weiler and the child is Andrew Gertig, sorry for switching it up and having the same first name!) You will be using your device.

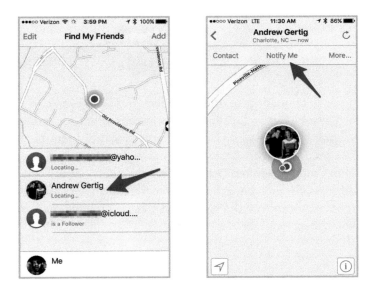

Tap on **Your Child's Name** (in this case, Andrew Gertig). On the next screen, tap **Notify Me.**

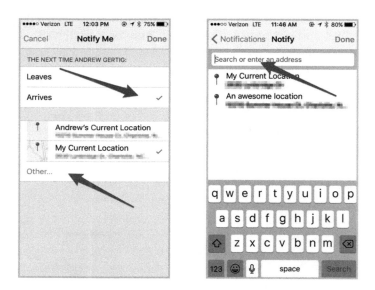

You can choose to be notified when your child either arrives or leaves a location. In this instance, let's assume we want to know when our child arrives at their stated destination. Tap on **Arrives** and make sure there is a check mark. Then tap **Other** to enter the destination address. Begin typing the location. If it is a known landmark, you can type the name and it will search the map, or you can enter a specific address.

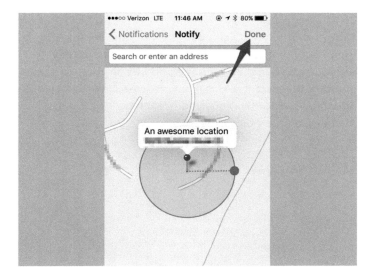

Once you have found the location, tap **Done**, and there you have it. When your child's device enters this radius, you will receive a notification. You can do this to be notified when they leave and again when they arrive at home.

One other note: if you want to set up recurring notifications, you can follow the instructions for **iOS 9** below, but use your child's device. In that example, tap on **Me.** On the following screen, tap on **Notify Friends** and then follow the instructions. It is a little more advanced. The above method is much simpler and equally effective.

CREATING A GEOFENCE NOTIFICATION IN IOS 9

Now that you have "**Friends**" you can now set up geofence notifications. To get started open **Find My Friends** on your child's iPhone and tap on your name (Reminder: the parent in this example is Andrew Gertig and the child is Andrew Weiler, sorry for having the same first name!) and then tap on **More**.

Then tap on **Notify Name** and then choose when you wish for the geofence notification to be triggered. Either **When I Leave** or **When I Arrive**. For this example, we will be setting a notification for when the child arrives at a predetermined location. This could be their school, the bus stop, or your home.

You can choose the location by tapping next to the Map icon with the pin. And lastly, before tapping **Done,** you will probably want to make sure that **Repeat Every Time** is turned on, but this is not mandatory.

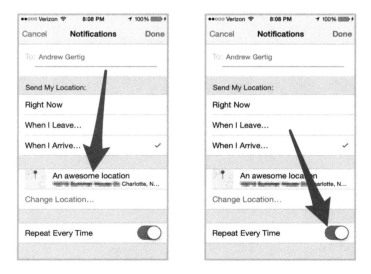

You have successfully created a **Geofence Notification**!

To see a list of all the notifications you have set up, you can tap on the **Me** button, then tap on **Notifications**.

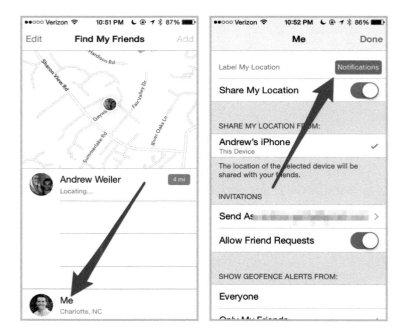

From this view you can delete notifications you have created or even add some more. Though we recommend adding them by the method we have outlined above.

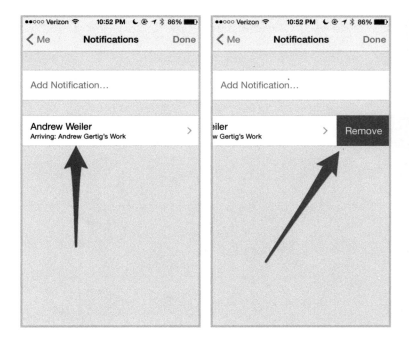

You are now a **Find My Friends** expert! Use this power wisely.

HOW TO

Share Purchases Using Family Sharing

The more connected we are to our technology, the more technology is keeping us better connected with each other. **Family Sharing** actually makes family life easier. There are several benefits including sharing and viewing purchases made by family members, requiring your kids to **Ask to Buy** any purchases, and even keeping a shared family calendar. Here are the simple steps you need to set up Family Sharing on all your devices.

GETTING UP TO DATE

First, update all your mobile devices to at least **iOS 8.0**, since Family Sharing does not work in **iOS 7**. Chances are very good that you are already running iOS 8 or greater, especially if you have purchased your device within the last 2 years. To make sure you have the correct version of iOS, tap **Settings** and then tap **General**. Next, tap **Software Update** and you will see if you have a pending update and what version you are running. If you are still running iOS 7 and have to update it may take a while so go make the kids lunches or rake a pile of leaves and come back to check.

SETTING UP FAMILY SHARING

Head back into **Settings** and tap **iCloud**. Tapping **iCloud** will take you to the family screen. Here you will be able to see your family members. Right now it will only show you as the **Organizer**. It will also show you the **Shared Payment Method** at the bottom. That is the credit card associated with your iCloud account. You can have other cards, but you need one shared card for all family members in order to share, and approve purchases.

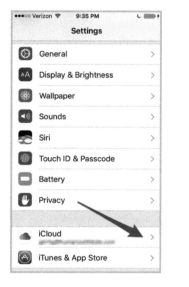 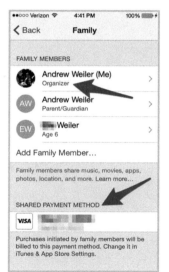

Next, it's time to add family members. To **Add Family Member** you need to know the email addresses of the other members of your family that are associated with their Apple account (their iTunes account for instance). When you enter the account name, it will prompt you for some credit card security information that verifies you are in charge of the account. If this is one of your accounts, you can enter the password to the account as well and you are good to go, that account is set up. If you are sending it to your spouse, you can just send the invitation that they can accept when they get the email.

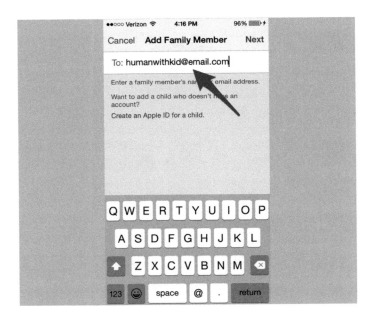

BUT, MY CHILD DOESN'T HAVE AN APPLE ID.

Apple requires you to be at least 13 to have your own account, but you can add a child under your **Family Sharing**. We recommend this, especially if you are considering giving your child a device of their own. This allows you to set up a lot of great parental features and controls, including making your children get your consent before purchasing any app or content from the App Store or iTunes.

From the **iCloud** screen, tap on **Family**, then swipe down and tap the small text that says **Create an Apple ID for a Child**. If you tap on the **Add Family Member**, it will take you to a screen where you will also see the text **Create an Apple ID for a Child**. Either way will do, we are just showing you one less tap. After tapping **Create an Apple ID for a Child** you will be taken you to a screen that will tell you a little about the policy. Read this and tap **Next**.

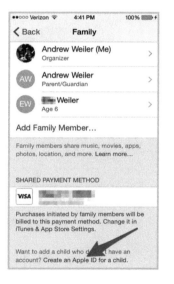

Then you will be asked to enter your child's birthdate. Once complete, it will take you to a screen about Apple's privacy policy. Important notes: Apple does not collect personally identifiable information, but it does collect data about usage and habits for targeted advertising within apps and browsing.

There is nothing unusual about this policy, but it can be a good conversation with your kids at some point that someone is always monitoring their web habits. We always recommend actually reading the policy to get an understanding of what is being collected and distributed, as well as the ways in which companies are working hard to protect your child's identity and information.

Next, you will be asked to verify the credit card associated with your account. Then you will be asked to give your child's name.

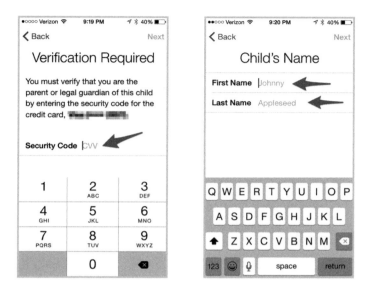

After that, you will create an email address for them, verify it, and on the following page, create a password.

Then, you will be given a set of security questions to select from and give answers. You will do this three times, with three different sets of questions. You will get the chance to turn on or off **Ask to Buy**. The default is on, and we recommend leaving it that way.

You will also be allowed to enter location sharing with family. If your child has their own device, we'd recommend using this feature so you know where they are easily. It only shares the location with the family, it won't be shared at large. Finally, you will be asked to agree to terms and conditions. At this point, you should receive an email saying that your child has been added to "Family Sharing."

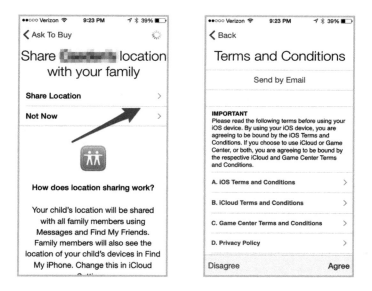

That's It! Congratulations, you have set up Family Sharing. See our post for a more detailed explanation of the benefits of family sharing. The short list is the ability to monitor and approve purchases, easily set restrictions on content, share purchases made from multiple accounts, see where everyone in your family is, and even manage a shared calendar.

RESTRICTIONS

Restrictions are a list of settings on your iPhone or iPad that you can disable to varying degrees, completely, or just prevent the current setting from being changed.

A bit of parent thought processing first. You need to know your kids. Know what they want, what they love, what they are tempted by, and where they are strong. Having every restriction on from the get go might not be the best idea, but having every one off only allows you to be punitive. There is great power in rewarding good behavior, so get to know all these restrictions and make some decisions on which ones you will always keep res tricted, and which can be earned by being a good steward of their device. It is never fun to feel like all you ever do is clamp down on your kids, ground them, and restrict them. Nevertheless, it is important to have some lines that you won't cross, values that you will hold even when they cause conflict. Don't get caught fighting worthless battles, but make a stand for what matters.

AGE 0-4

Your child can use designated apps, like Preschool Farm Fun, for education and entertainment. We recommend limiting any device usage to 15 minutes or less at a time and no more than 30 minutes in a day. It's a good idea to have some restrictions set up just in case your child taps buttons at random and ends up somewhere dangerous.

AGE 5-8

Your child may begin using a device and navigating it on their own. We still recommend a very limited time of use, and we recommend that for any online activity they be accompanied by an adult. This is the age to make sure to start enabling restrictions when your child is using a mobile device.

AGE 9-12

Your child will be interested in using social media. Internet use has become more regular and technology use is often implemented and encouraged at school. This is the time to make sure you have good search filters on, and make sure that restrictions are in place. If you have not begun the conversation about using the internet responsibly, make sure to do so towards the beginning of this age range. This is the time that many kids accidentally find or see content that they should not see. Also, this is often the time that parents allow their children to get a social networking identity. Almost all popular social media sites do not allow users under 13. Don't be tempted to cheat the system. You don't want to be the parent that okays lying about age on the internet. That is a dangerous precedent to set. Also, your child may develop a real desire to understand gaming and how computers work. We encourage you to start helping your kids learn to code at this age. They are ready to succeed at basic coding now, and the ability to read and write computer code will be an invaluable skill to grow up with.

AGE 13-15

Social media use is ubiquitous. You should find a way that works for your family to introduce the use of social media in your home. Lay the groundwork for open and honest communication as well as the precedent of transparency. Also, bring your kids into the discussion about tech use at home and allow them to both help make the rules and enforce them. Make sure that you, as a parent, conform to the rules of your house. Limit your own screen time. A good rule of thumb that we have heard is that every day you should have one hour of no touching a screen, every week you should have one day of no screen use, and every year you should commit to one week of no screen usage. At this age, your kids are becoming independent. You should focus more on responsible behavior than punitive actions and hard boundaries. Eventually, they will have no boundaries, so it is time to prepare them for that day by limiting some of the restrictions.

AGE 16-18

They are almost free. Other than a few filters for sexually graphic content (which we recommend for even adults) the limits should now be only enforced when behavior is not managed by your child. Make sure that you clearly lay out the expectations for their behavior and allow them to meet your expectations. This is like driving. You no longer have complete control, so don't wait until this point to teach them how to control themselves; it will be too difficult to enforce or correct.

Restrictions allow you to have some level of control over what happens on a device before it actually happens. For yourself, this may allow you to keep from accidentally or intentionally viewing material you find offensive. For other devices that you own, but are being used by other members of your family, restrictions allow you to limit content, location sharing, app purchases, and even the use of selected apps.

Go into the **Settings** app. Under the settings menu tap on

General, then scroll down to **Restrictions**. Remember, this **Restrictions Passcode** should not be the same passcode as your device unlock passcode. Here are all the settings and what they do.

ENABLE/DISABLE RESTRICTIONS

This will toggle on or off all the restrictions listed below. If you turn this On you will need to enter a Passcode. Make sure the Passcode is different than your unlock passcode. All restrictions are turned on or off via this toggle switch.

A Restrictions passcode is a 4 digit number (or longer!) that allows you to control many of the restriction setting on an iOS device. This code is different than the unlock code, known as the Passcode, and if you want to control access, you should make sure it is actually a different numerical code.

Follow these steps to access the restriction settings and set up a passcode. If you need a deeper walkthrough on how to do this, check out our recipe: *How to Lock the Settings on your iPhone or iPad.*

Step 1

From the Home Screen, tap on the **Settings** icon and enter the settings panel.

Step 2

Scroll down and tap on **General** and scroll down to find **Restrictions** and tap on it. If you have not set up **Restrictions** it will have an Off label on the right.

Step 3

Enable Restrictions. At the top you will see a row that says **Enable Restrictions.** When you tap on it, a menu will appear that allows you to set up a **Restrictions Passcode**. Enter your passcode now, making sure that it is not the same as your unlock passcode. You will be asked to re-enter the passcode to verify it. If you are successful, it will return you to the Restrictions page and you will see **Disable Restrictions**. Additionally, all of the rows below will no longer be grayed out and you will be able to adjust settings for apps and content.

––––––––––––––––––

This toggles on or off the use of Safari. Safari is Apple's internet browser. It is important to note that Safari is not the only browser available for a mobile device. There are literally hundreds of different browsers, so don't be fooled into thinking that if you turn this off that the device will not be able to connect to the internet. It just means that you can't use Safari to do so. Any other browser on the phone will still access the internet. The only way to control other browsers is to eliminate them from the device and make sure that downloads are not allowed. Restricting websites will work across any browsers installed on your phone, so you can manage and limit content (See the "How to Restrict Explicit Content").

––––––––––––––––––

You can toggle on or off the use of the camera on the device. Turning this off automatically turns off FaceTime as well.

––––––––––––––––––

Siri is a voice recognizing assistant in your phone. You can talk to her and she will respond, follow commands and search the web. Dictation allows you to tap a small button that looks like a microphone on your keyboard to dictate written content. This switch turns either of these features on or off.

FaceTime is Apple's proprietary video chat. It allows you to see the person you are talking to from your device. This switch toggles on or off the use of FaceTime.

AirDrop is Apple's Bluetooth enabled local file sharing application. AirDrop allows you to share any file, photos, videos, or documents with people who are nearby and also have AirDrop enabled. This switch turns AirDrop on or off.

CarPlay is a new update for Apple and will likely become increasingly popular if you have a CarPlay enabled Car Stereo. CarPlay connects to your phone directly and allows you to stay safe while interacting with your phone in the car. We have not used this feature, but the concept seems to be beneficial for iPhone users to stay safer in the car. This switch turns CarPlay on or off.

This switch will toggle the iTunes music store on and off. This is where you would go to buy music, movies, and TV shows. When you turn the iTunes Store off, it actually removes the icon on your device and you can't see it at all. It also removes the Store tab in your iTunes music app (located in the top left corner). Additionally, it removes the

Store tab in the Videos app as well. One thing to notice: if you have the iTunes store in a folder when you turn off iTunes store it will not return there when you turn the store back on. Instead, it will return to your home screen.

This switch will toggle the Apple Music Connect on and off. Apple Music is a subscription streaming service that allows you to download or stream music from your device. You can set up a single membership or share one across your entire family. Turning off Apple Music Connect does not remove it from your device, nor does it remove already downloaded music or the ability to stream music. Apple Music Connect allow you to follow and interact with lifestyle conversations and features by select artists. Toggling this switch off simply removes the social media aspects of Apple Music Connect, not any other feature of Apple Music. Be sure to double check your ratings for Music if you want to limit content.

This switch toggles the iBooks store on or off. This switch turns on or off the ability to search the iBooks store and find new material. When off you can still access the iBooks app and read anything that is in your library, whether it is downloaded on your device or not. This means that if you have a book that you have purchased, it will be accessible even if the iBooks store is turned off. Inside of iBooks you can hide books that are on the iCloud. This is not a restricted switch so your child could access any book that is shared on the iCloud if they know how.

This switch removes the entire podcast app from your iPad. You cannot access, download or even listen to a podcast when this switch is off. Like the iTunes Store, when you turn podcasts back on, the app returns on your home screen, not in any folder to which it was previously added.

This switch will toggle the News App on and off. When off, the News App is completely hidden from your phone and no news stories will show up in your notifications screen.

This switch removes the entire App Store app from your device. You cannot search for or download any apps at all. This also disables external links to the App Store, so if you are surfing the web and a site asks if you want to download their app, the link will only take you to a blank page since the App Store is disabled.

When it is on, you can delete apps, but when it is off, you cannot delete them. When deleting apps is off and you hold your finger over an app, all the app icons wiggle, but they don't show the little x in the top left corner allowing to delete them. They still can be moved around and into folders, but not deleted. This is handy when your device is in the hands of a younger child that hasn't mastered all the interfaces yet and sometimes moves and deletes your apps.

This switch disables the purchase of items or subscriptions inside an app. This includes games that ask you to purchase extra items as well as services that require a premium subscription. This is a great feature to leave on so no one in your household accidentally purchases more than they intend to purchase.

———————————

Each country has a different rating system for content. For example in the United States TV ratings have 6 categories ranging from TV-Y to TV-MA, while in the United Kingdom they only have one category called CAUTION. This setting allows you to select which country's rating system you would like to use. By default it is preset for the country you purchased the device in.

———————————

The default is set to allow explicit language. If you would like to turn off any explicit music, podcasts or other content, slide this switch off. This will also hide the downloaded content from your iTunes app that is rated Explicit so little ears don't accidentally hear things you don't want them to be hearing

———————————

This brings you to another screen where you can select which Movie ratings you want allowed on this device. You can select a graduated series of movies from allow no movies through all ratings G to NC-17 or simply allow all movies. If you have movies accessible on your device, we strongly recommend using this system to prevent your children accessing something that you would rather them not see at their current age.

———————————

This brings you to another screen, like with Movies, where you have a range of options to select. It contains all the

TV ratings from TV-Y all the way to TV-MA, as well as the option to allow all TV shows or no TV shows. If you download TV from the iTunes store, we also highly recommend using this setting to keep your children from seeing things before you are ready for them to see those things.

This switch toggles explicit sexual content. If it is switched on, explicit sexual content is available. Turned off, there is no access to that type of content. That is the only rating for books, so you must monitor written content and reading choices.

There are two switches for Siri, Apple's voice activated assistant. The first switch toggles whether or not Siri types out explicit content. When limiting explicit content, Siri will type back words with asterisks in place of some letters. It does not limit what you say as a prompt for Siri. Generally, Siri does not actively use explicit language, but undoubtedly there are ways to trick Siri into saying something crass.

The second switch toggles whether or not Siri is permitted to search the web. This is a real valuable tool. When off, Siri responds as not permitted to search the web for you. This is a good add on protection for limiting content and web search capabilities that you'd like to limit.

When a developer submits an app to the App Store they are required to choose an age range for the app. This is then reviewed by Apple for accuracy but is not a guarantee that the content is in fact age appropriate. For example, if you wish for your child to only be able to access apps that are rated as 4+, you should ensure only that option is selected.

This gives you three settings. The first is to allow any and all websites, the second limits adult content and the third allows only specific websites that you choose. When you select this, it shows a set of preloaded websites that are automatically allowed. You can add websites to this list or delete them by selecting each site individually and deleting the name and URL. When you navigate to a restricted page, it will allow you the option of allowing the website, but the user must have the passcode. This is one of the reasons why your restrictions passcode must be different than your unlock passcode. For young children, we recommend only allowing a few websites, but as they get older and need access for school, it may be best to allow them access, but simply limit adult content. This method will not be foolproof, but it is difficult to keep up with sites that may be needed for information and research for school. Also, this restriction will work across multiple browsers, including within social media apps like Facebook and Twitter. It will not limit the content populating their newsfeeds, but it will prohibit access to the site when clicking on a link.

PRIVACY

Privacy has become a topic that many parents aren't used to worrying about. In the technology connected world, our usage is recorded, our preferences and likes are shared or sold, and our locations are tracked. Most of the time the usage of this data is either benign to us or even beneficial. However, our children need us to be thinking about their privacy because they are not naturally inclined to think about the consequences of sharing everything. While you should be carefully considering the apps your child uses and the age at which they use them (Facebook, for instance, doesn't technically allow users under age 13), there are good reasons to actually think through what data is shared about yourself and your child. Most apps that keep data on a child keep only metadata, that is usage information, not personally identifying data. Nonetheless, it is you who are responsible for your family and that means setting the boundaries for which data is accessible to apps, the world of advertisers, educators, friends, and relatives.

To access the **Privacy** settings tap on the **Settings** app icon on the Home Screen, then scroll down and tap on **Privacy**.

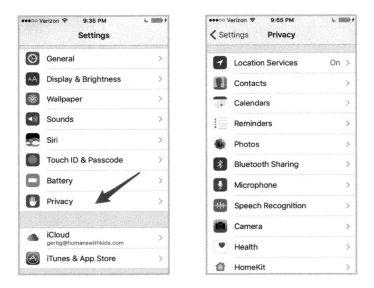

The list under **Location Services** contains many of the services and data centers on your phone. If you select any of the tabs like, **Contacts** or below, it will give you the list of any third party app that has asked for and been granted access to the data contained within that app. This is a good reminder to check things like **Camera** and **Photos**, and even **Microphone** every so often to be sure that you know what other applications have access to your data.

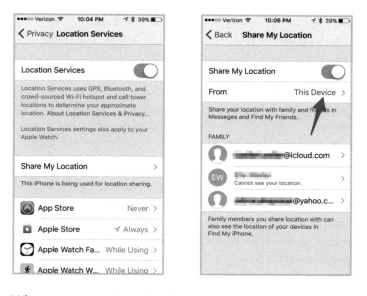

When you tap on **Location Services** you get to a screen where you are able to select whether you enable **Location Services** at all. While it is tempting to hide from the world, there are many benefits to sharing your location. There is a list of apps that are accessing your location. Tapping on any of the apps in that list allows you to toggle between sharing your location **Always**, **Never,** or **While Using**. This allows you to pick and choose what you want to share and with whom you wish to share it. Additionally, tapping on the **Share My Location** tab brings up the second screen. The allows you to decide whether you wish to share your location with others of your friends and family. It also allows you to decide from which device you share your location. This is a good note for anyone who has multiple devices tied to the same Apple ID. If your child has an iPhone and an iPad for instance, they may be able to switch which one is showing your their location. Just worth checking in on every now and then if you are concerned.

All of your devices, when connected, are capable of knowing where you are. This can be a great asset when you are using a Maps app or trying to locate a nearby restaurant. Some apps only use this service while you are actively using the app, and it is open. Others are collecting that data even when you are not directly using the app. This might be fine for you as an adult, but if the device belongs to your child, you may not want them automatically sharing where they are all the time.

There are numerous apps out there that want access to your location. Several, like Camera and Reminders, are part of the iOS operating system and many more you can download from the App Store. Apps must always ask for permission to access your location and there are two ways apps can access your location once you have given them permission to do so: **Always** or **While Using the App**. These are fairly self descriptive and it is up to the app which of these, or both, to request. Any app that has access to your location can be denied that access by tapping on the app's name in this list and tapping on Never.

We highly recommend that you tap on Camera and tap on **Never**. Why? Because if not, then every time your child takes a picture on their phone, it is tagged with the location and time that the picture was taken. Then what happens to those pictures? They get uploaded to somewhere like Facebook or Instagram and then it is very easy for someone to find out where your child is right now by looking at the meta data of that picture.

We highly recommend that you do a thorough review of the apps that have access to your location. We advise you to set any photo or video taking application to **Never**.

<hr />

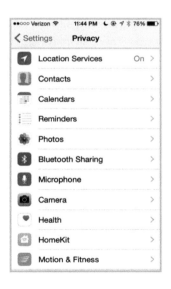

The **Privacy** categories list apps that have requested access to that feature or setting. If an app shows up inside one of these categories, it is because you explicitly gave it permission to do so. You may be looking at the long list of apps in a category like Photos and are wondering "When did that happen!" Yes, we know, it's very easy to just click "Okay" whenever you see a popup. Going through this list is a great exercise to help remind you what apps have access to which areas of your phone.

Contacts, **Calendars and Reminders** - apps that have access to these categories read, edit, update, and delete. That means these apps can know the phone numbers and email addresses of all of your contacts and can upload them to a web server without your knowledge. They can also make changes to your Calendar and read the details of any event.

Photos - any app that has access to your Photos can upload your full photo library and can also read any metadata from any photo, such as what time the photo was taken, and the location it was taken in if you have not disabled Location on your Photos.

Bluetooth Sharing - this is not a common category. It is used by apps that want to share data with each other via Bluetooth.

Microphone - Apple requires apps that take video to request access to the Microphone. Apple does not allow apps to record audio in the background without displaying a large Red banner at the top of your screen. Hard to miss! If an app requests access to your Microphone but does not record audio or video, then you should be cautious.

Camera - Most apps that request access to your photos also request access the camera. You might think these should be the same thing but they are not. An app cannot use the camera on your device without first getting your permission.

Health, HomeKit, Motion & Fitness - these are relatively new categories and many apps are not yet using these features. Apps that have access to these categories can do things like read the number of steps you have taken or read from data that you have input into the Health app.

Twitter and Facebook - apps have the ability to log you in using your Twitter or Facebook credentials that you may have stored on your phone in the built in apps. They can then use this data to get data from these services and take action on your behalf.

Diagnostics & Usage - This is purely for Apple. It is up to you whether you send data back to Apple or not. Apple is very clear that they do not collect data off of your device without your permission. As App Developers ourselves (Preschool Farm Fun on the iPad!), we love it when people turn on Share With App Developers but that's totally up to you.

Advertising - the only real option here is to turn on Limit Ad Tracking. If you turn this off, then Apple will not tailor its ads to you. Pretty much a toss-up here. You still get ads.

CONCLUSION

Parenting is like creating a circle within which our kids learn to make good decisions. Outside the circle, we as parents, make the choices for them. Inside the circle, they have freedom to decide what to do and who they are going to be. The edge needs to be far enough out that they feel empowered to decide some meaningful things in their lives, but not so open that they can get hurt badly. The difficult job of parenting is expanding and contracting that circle so that we always have the optimal edge for both kids and parents. One day they need to function in a world in which they are responsible for all of their own decisions. After all, we aren't raising kids, we are raising adults. It is our sincere hope that this book gives you the tools you need to help move that boundary appropriately, effectively, and at the time you see fit as it relates to your child and the ever-present devices in our lives.

In many ways, our iPhones and iPads have made our lives easier, but they also bring new challenges. It is also true that technology is not slowing down. There are going to be quantum leaps in the way our kids will use technology, as revolutionary as the airplane or the internal combustion engine. Our kids will end up being comfortable with these devices, and we need to be able to meet them with wisdom as they grow. The goal for this book was to equip you with the knowledge you need to confidently allow the use of these devices by your children. Understanding the tools we use is just as important with our technology as it is with, say, the car that we drive. We don't need to be a mechanic, but we need to know the basics of driving safely. Our intent is that this book would feel more like driver's ed and less like a manual for an aspiring mechanic. We hope you have learned something new and feel better equipped to do your sacred job as a parent.

Thank you very much for reading this book.

Please be sure to check out our website at http://humanswithkids.com and sign up for our monthly newsletter. We would also love for you to send us any feedback you have at hello@humanswithkids.com and if you bought this book on Amazon, please leave us a review, it really helps!

Thanks!

Andrew Gertig and Andrew Weiler

Andrew Weiler   Andrew Gertig

ABOUT THE AUTHORS

Andrew Weiler, co-founder of Humans with Kids, is a former children's minister and self-proclaimed pirate. He drinks coffee and does all kinds of stuff in Charlotte, NC with his crew of wife Amy and two kids Elle and Caeden.

Andrew Gertig, co-founder of Humans with Kids, is an iPhone and iPad app developer and a constant tinkerer. He has regular tea parties in Charlotte, NC with his wife Amanda, their two kids William and Kathryn, and of course their dog Stella, too.